FUSION

LIFE OF A SODA CAN

by Louise Nelson

BEARPORT
PUBLISHING

Minneapolis, Minnesota

Credits

Front cover – Littlekidmoment, OlegDoroshin, Chake. 3 – sunstock/iStock. 4&5 – Akimov Igor, Bauwimauwi. 6&7 – Roman Samokhin, Maksim_Gusev. 8&9 – Ann in the uk, Steve Allen. 10&11 – vchal, Tom Grundy. 11 – jat306/iStock. 12&13 – Rawpixel.com, Artur_eM. 14&15 – siam.pukkato, Paul Vasarhelyi, Cultura Motion, sunsetman, Ian Walsh. 16&17 – Vershinin89, MOLPIX. 18&19 – ppart, kongsky, taviphoto, Kletr, Anton Starikov, Oleksiy Mark, leshun irina, Winai Tepsuttinun. 20&21 – uanhuongho, Nichola Chapman, Fadila Suryandika, deannalindsey, elisa galceran garcia. 22&23 – Littlekidmoment, cinarlarinenes, Don Pablo, Maksim_Gusev, Bauwimauwi. Images are courtesy of Shutterstock.com. With thanks to Getty Images, Thinkstock Photo, and iStockphoto.

Library of Congress Cataloging-in-Publication Data is available at www.loc.gov or upon request from the publisher.

ISBN: 978-1-63691-902-7 (hardcover)
ISBN: 978-1-63691-907-2 (paperback)
ISBN: 978-1-63691-912-6 (ebook)

© 2023 Booklife Publishing
This edition is published by arrangement with Booklife Publishing.

North American adaptations © 2023 Bearport Publishing Company. All rights reserved. No part of this publication may be reproduced in whole or in part, stored in any retrieval system, or transmitted in any form or by any means, electronic, mechanical, photocopying, recording, or otherwise, without written permission from the publisher.

For more information, write to Bearport Publishing, 5357 Penn Avenue South, Minneapolis, MN 55419. Printed in the United States of America.

Contents

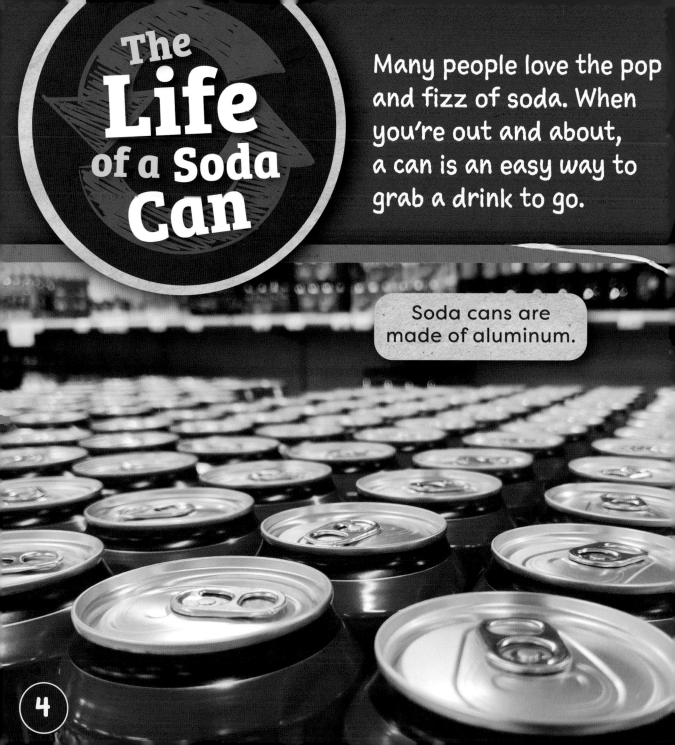

The Life of a Soda Can

Many people love the pop and fizz of soda. When you're out and about, a can is an easy way to grab a drink to go.

Soda cans are made of aluminum.

Do you know what happens to a can when you are done with it?

Every year, people around the world use about 180 billion aluminum cans.

What Is Aluminum?

Aluminum is a **metal**. It is strong, but it is not heavy. This metal is often smooth and shiny.

Aluminum can be made into many shapes.

Aluminum forms **underground**. But that does not mean we find metal cans in the earth.

Before we can use aluminum, we must melt it.

A Single Use

Soda cans are made to be used once. You can't use them over and over. They are single-use items.

You can't close a can back up once it has been opened.

So, what can you do with cans after their one use? You can throw cans away, or you can **recycle** them.

Trashing Cans

If you throw your can in the garbage, it will go to a **landfill**. This is a huge pit full of trash. Landfills are bad for the **environment**.

There are thousands of landfills across North America.

A can in the landfill will sit there for a long time. Then, even more aluminum needs to be used to make new cans.

An aluminum can may stay in a landfill for hundreds of years.

What Is Recycling?

Instead of the garbage, put your can into a recycling bin. This gives the can a new life.

Soda cans are recycled with a lot of other metal items.

Soda cans are recycled into new cans over and over again!

Recycling is when we turn old, used things into new things. We can recycle old aluminum cans into new ones.

Recycling a Soda Can

Once your soda can is empty, rinse it with water to make sure it is clean.

Find the right recycling bin for your can.

PAPER

PLASTIC

CANS

Different places may recycle differently. In some spots, you need to **sort** your soda cans into groups called metal or can recycling.

Recycling pickup at home

In the park

At school

At a recycling center

PLASTIC

PAPER

CA

15

Inside a Recycling Center

Then, aluminum cans go to the recycling center. There, they are cut into small pieces and melted.

Melted aluminum is reshaped into something new.

The recycled aluminum is just as good as new aluminum. But it takes a lot less **energy** to make it into something new.

Aluminum can be recycled forever, again and again.

17

Trash to Treasure

Most soda cans are made into new cans. But they are also made into other things.

Aluminum foil

A dishwasher

Food packaging

A **reusable** bottle

Car parts

Wire

A ladder

A bike

It is much easier to use recycled aluminum than to find new metal and melt it down.

19

Reuse and Upcycle

A soda can may only be used once for a drink. But this doesn't mean you have to put it straight in the recycling.

Can you reuse your can for something else?

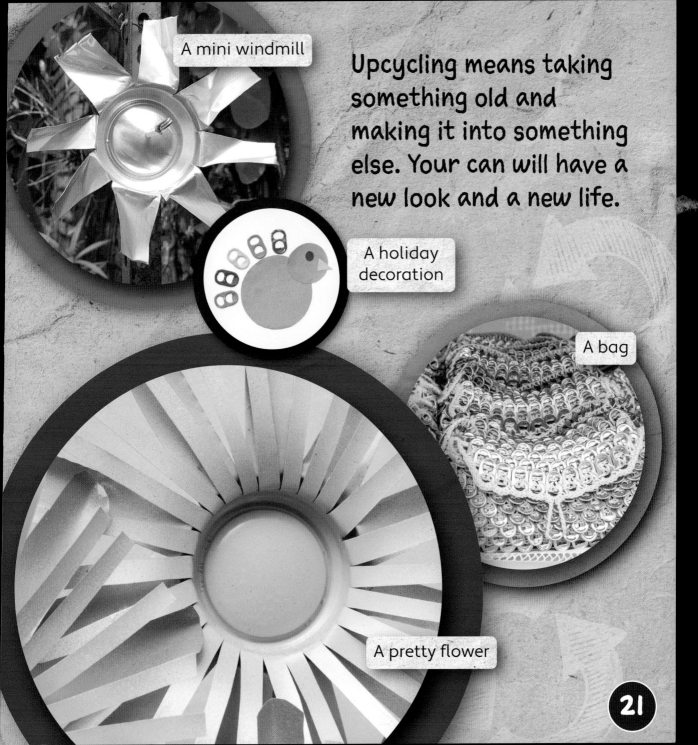

A mini windmill

Upcycling means taking something old and making it into something else. Your can will have a new look and a new life.

A holiday decoration

A bag

A pretty flower

21

The Eco Journey of a Soda Can

The aluminum is ready to become something new.

A can is bought and used.

The pieces are melted.

When it's empty, the can is washed and recycled.

Cans are cut into pieces at the recycling center.

Quick Quiz

Can you remember the eco journey of a soda can? Let's see! Look back through the book if you can't remember.

1. What are soda cans made of?
a) Steel
b) Plastic
c) Aluminum

2. How long might a can stay in a landfill?
a) One year
b) Hundreds of years
c) Thousands of years

3. How many times can a can be recycled into another can?
a) Forever
b) Once or twice
c) Cans can't be recycled

4. Which of these is not true about aluminum?
a) It is smooth
b) It is fluffy
c) It is shiny

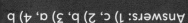

Glossary

energy power used to make something work or happen

environment the natural world

landfill a large hole in the ground used for dumping garbage

metal a hard, strong material found in the ground

recycle to collect, sort, and treat waste so it is turned into something that can be used again

reusable something that can be used many times

sort to arrange according to type

underground below the surface of Earth

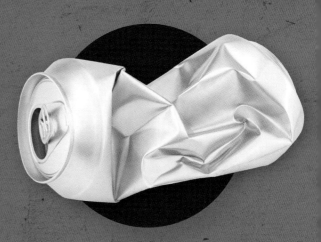

Index